Pebble® Plus

Earth and Space Science

The Water Cycle

by Craig Hammersmith

CAPSTONE PRESS
a capstone imprint

Pebble Plus is published by Capstone Press,
1710 Roe Crest Drive, North Mankato, Minnesota 56003.
www.capstonepub.com

Library of Congress Cataloging-in-Publication Data
Hammersmith, Craig.
  The water cycle / by Craig Hammersmith.
    p. cm. — (Pebble plus: Earth and space science)
  Includes bibliographical references and index.
  Summary: "Simple text and full-color photos explain the science behind the water cycle"—Provided by publisher.
  ISBN 978-1-4296-6812-5 (library binding) — ISBN 978-1-4296-7142-2 (paperback)
  1. Hydrologic cycle—Juvenile literature. I. Title.
  GB848.H366 2012
  551.48—dc22   2011005136

Editorial Credits
Gillia Olson, editor; Lori Bye, designer; Wanda Winch, media researcher; Laura Manthe, production specialist

Photo Credits
Capstone, 18; Capstone Studio: Karon Dubke, 20, 21 (all); iStockphoto: erikwkolstad, 9, ideeone, cover, rodho, 1; Shutterstock: Dainia Derics, 15, IntraClique LLC, 17, Nata-Lia, 11 (bottom), Nikolajs Lunskijs, 19, Pi-Lens, 11 (top), pixelparticle, 5, SebStock, 7; Superstock Inc.: Beyond, 13

Note to Parents and Teachers

The Earth and Space Science series supports national science standards related to earth and space science. This book describes and illustrates the water cycle. The images support early readers in understanding the text. The repetition of words and phrases helps early readers learn new words. This book also introduces early readers to subject-specific vocabulary words, which are defined in the Glossary section. Early readers may need assistance to read some words and to use the Table of Contents, Glossary, Read More, Internet Sites, and Index sections of the book.

Printed in the United States of America in Stevens Point, Wisconsin.
082013   007677R

Table of Contents

Recycled Water

The water now on Earth

is the same water

that has always been here.

Luckily, nature recycles water

using the water cycle.

The First Step

Evaporation is the first step in the water cycle. The sun heats liquid water. The water changes into a gas called water vapor. The vapor rises into the air.

Making Clouds

Up high, the vapor meets cold air and cools. It turns back into liquid water droplets or freezes into ice crystals. This process is condensation.

Condensation forms clouds.
High, thin cirrus clouds are
made from ice crystals.
Low, puffy cumulus clouds are
full of water droplets.

cirrus clouds

cumulus clouds

Coming Down

The water droplets or ice crystals in a cloud can get too heavy to stay in the air. They then fall to the ground. This process is precipitation.

Precipitation falls in many forms.

Rain is liquid water.

It falls when the air is warm.

Snow is frozen ice crystals.

It falls when the air is freezing.

Sleet and hail are precipitation.
Sleet goes from frozen to liquid
to frozen again before hitting
the ground. Raindrops freeze
in the air to form balls of hail.

Once precipitation falls,

the water cycle begins again.

Nature is a great recycler!

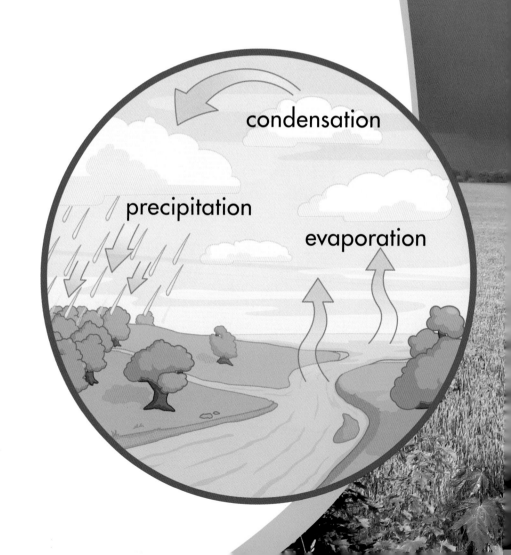

Make a Terrarium

A terrarium is a small, covered container where you can see a water cycle.

You will need:
- small plastic cup
- small gravel or coarse sand
- a large jar with a lid
- potting soil
- small tropical plants like ferns
- water

With the lid on the terrarium, all of the water that is poured on the plants will evaporate, condense, and then fall back on the plants over and over again!

1. Put a cup of gravel or sand in the jar.
2. Add two cups of potting soil.
3. Put in two or three plants.
4. Water the plants so the soil is wet. Put on the lid.

Glossary

condensation—the act of changing from a gas to a liquid

evaporation—the act of turning from a liquid to a gas

hail—balls of ice that form in clouds and fall to the ground

precipitation—water that falls from clouds to the Earth's surface in the form of rain, snow, sleet, or hail

recycle—the process of turning something old into something new

sleet—precipitation that hits the ground as tiny balls of frozen ice

water vapor—water in the form of a gas

Read More

Kalman, Bobbie. *Water Changes*. My World. New York: Crabtree Pub., 2011.

Koontz, Robin. *Water Goes Round: The Water Cycle*. Nature Cycles. Mankato, Minn.: Capstone Press, 2011.

Slade, Suzanne. *A Raindrop's Journey*. Follow It! Mankato, Minn.: Picture Window Books, 2011.

Internet Sites

FactHound offers a safe, fun way to find Internet sites related to this book. All of the sites on FactHound have been researched by our staff.

Here's all you do:

Visit *www.facthound.com*

Type in this code: 9781429668125

Super-cool stuff! Check out projects, games and lots more at **www.capstonekids.com**

Index

Word Count: 194
Grade: 1
Early-Intervention Level: 23